C000301406

FLYING AND BALLOONING
from old photographs

Flying and Ballooning

from old photographs

Introduction and commentaries by
JOHN FABB

B.T. BATSFORD LTD · LONDON

By the same author
VICTORIAN AND EDWARDIAN ARMY
from old photographs

with A.C. McGowan
VICTORIAN AND EDWARDIAN NAVY

First published 1980
Text copyright © John Fabb 1980
Filmset in 'Monophoto' Souvenir by
Servis Filmsetting Ltd, Manchester
Printed in Great Britain by
The Anchor Press, Tiptree, Essex

for the publishers B.T. Batsford Ltd,
4 Fitzhardinge Street, London W1H 0AH
ISBN 0 7134 2015 4

1 *Frontispiece* A balloon about to ascend from 'The Mount', Batheaston, Somerset, the home of Patrick Alexander

Contents

ACKNOWLEDGMENTS The Author and Publishers would like to thank the following for permission to reproduce their photographs in this book: Canterbury Public Library (2); The Imperial War Museum (7, 8, 10, 28, 30, 31, 56, 58, 62, 66, 89, 92, 94, 104, 106, 108, 112); The Kodak Museum (22, 23, 24, 25, 34, 64, 76, 103, 105, 107, 113); Ministry of Defence, Farnborough (27, 69, 82); National Army Museum (3, 9, 17, 44, 45, 46, 47, 48, 49, 50, 51, 52, 53, 54, 57, 80, 86, 87); The Science Museum (33, 65, 70, 81, 84, 85, 88, 90); Tonbridge Historical Society (96); photograph nos. 19, 21, 83 and 99 are from the Publishers' collection. The remaining photographs are from the Author's collection.

Introduction

One of man's earliest ambitions was to leave the ground and fly, but it was not until the eighteenth, and to a greater extent the nineteenth century that this dream was finally fulfilled.

The great public interest in ballooning and flying was reflected in the number of prints and paintings that appeared in those centuries. By the time photography was practicable, ballooning had become a regular pastime. Movement could not be recorded until the experiments of Dr Richard Maddox in 1871 led to the fast gelatine silver bromide plate that was developed by Charles Bennett, John Burgess and Richard Kennett. In 1873 Burgess made the first gelatine dry plates for sale. Whereas wet collodion plates had to be used immediately after their sensitisation, the dry plates, brought ready prepared, could be kept for long periods before using. This advance allowed the photographer greater freedom in the use of his camera. Outside events such as ballooning and flying could be covered. Pictures were generally made on albumen paper until the 1890s, when gelatine silver chloride or bromide paper became generally available.

In the late 1880s gelatine emulsion could be coated on a celluloid roll film, which gave the photographer even greater freedom in the choice of subject and mobility in recording it.

Regrettably, no one photographer specialised in capturing the activities of the balloonists. The novelty of flying made it a suitable subject for all photographers. Unfortunately from our point of view, flying was looked upon as a scientific study and the bulk of pictures available are of a static piece of machinery without the human and social interest that makes early photographs so interesting. Official pictures abound, but again these are static. A considerable number of the photographs illustrated in this book were taken by the popular box cameras introduced in the 1890s. Easy to carry and to operate at a moment's notice they allowed any number of subjects to be photographed with a more realistic result. Magazines are a fruitful source of old photographs. Such periodicals as *The Bystander*, *The Tatler*, *The Illustrated London News* and *The Graphic* depicted flying and ballooning on social occasions, and also when the subject was newsworthy; which at the turn of the century began to be more often.

Libraries are also an invaluable source of pictures. Librarians are generally interested in their district and have built up a good selection of local photographs which may include balloons or aircraft. That area of research is of course immense, and it would need a great deal of time to explore thoroughly the vast potential that exists in libraries.

A number of the pictures in this book have never before been seen in print, and others not since the first time the photograph was taken, because they have been stored away and forgotten for many years as no longer newsworthy.

One of the difficulties incidental to finding a good photograph is the inability to discover exactly where and what it represents; a good deal of detective work is required. Dating is difficult because we are only concerned with the period from the 1840s up to about 1912. The style of clothes, although subject to constant changes in high fashion, did not filter down so quickly to the man or woman in the street. Thus a date of say 1880 can cover ten years, quite a long time. Luckily flying and ballooning were such a novel experience that dating becomes easier. The photographs and the people who developed and flew these machines were celebrities. A number of them are still widely remembered today, for example Colonel Cody and the Hon. C.S. Rolls.

But there are many photographs of ordinary enthusiastic people who found ballooning and flying an exciting experience. For ladies ballooning was a sport in which they could participate and in which the dictates of current fashion were not a disability. Many photographs in this book depict these ladies in flight, at first as balloonists, and later, with the advent of the flying machines, in heavier than air machines also.

British military aeronautics began in 1878 at Woolwich under Captain J.L.B. Templer with a grant of £150.00. As usual, governments dragged their feet and all early ballooning and flying was subsidised out of the enthusiastic officers' pockets.

A balloon was used in the 1879 review at Dover and again at Brighton in 1880. In the same year, balloon training was initiated at Aldershot with the Royal Engineers. Gold beaters' skin, which was prepared from the lower membranes of an ox, was more impervious to hydrogen, as well as being lighter and stronger than other materials. A photograph of this operation is illustrated (7).

In 1885 a balloon detachment was employed under Major Elsdale during the Bechuanaland expedition, and under Major Templer in the Red Sea and Eastern Sudan War. In the Sudan a lack of transport and gas seriously hampered balloon operations and few positive results were obtained.

Other aerial activities included the experiments in air photography carried out by Major Elsdale, who sent up small balloons carrying automatic cameras. He had started this when stationed in Halifax, Nova Scotia, Canada in 1883, taking some successful photographs of the Fort from the air. Balloons had limited use in the South African war in 1899, at gun spotting and reconnaissance, but after the end of the Boer Army proper, the guerilla nature of operations made the use of balloons impracticable.

Colonel S.F. Cody, whose photograph appears in the book (76), was employed in the Army Balloon factory from 1904, on the construction of kites. He was an American citizen until he became a naturalised British subject in 1909. He was killed in 1913 whilst testing a new machine.

As with the balloon, the British Government was slow to realise the potential of heavier than air machines, and it was not until 1910 that the War Office announced the expansion of the balloon section to include flying machines. The Air Battalion was formed six months later and included expert air officers and men. Until then there was no general demand for air employment and the handling of the balloons and machines had been left to the Royal Engineers.

On 13 May 1912, the Royal Flying Corps (Military Wing) was officially inaugurated, taking over from the Air Battalion Royal Engineers, and absorbing the bulk of the personnel. The Naval Wing soon became the Royal Naval Air Service and the designation 'Military Wing' became obsolete. In 1914 all airship work became the prerogative of the Royal Navy.

A final word may be given by General Sir W.S. Nicholson, Chief of the Imperial General Staff, who in 1900 stated that flying was 'A useless and expensive fad, advocated by a few individuals whose ideas are unworthy of attention'.

2 The 'Colonel' balloon, preparing to take Colonel Brine on his first Channel trip from Canterbury, 1882

Balloons

3 The Balloon Section of the Royal Engineers receiving instructions on Balloon handling, 1893

4 To celebrate the first balloon ascent from the City of Bath in 1802, a balloon carrying two men, Professor Gaudron and Mr Poole, ascended from Sydney Gardens, Bath in 1902. The balloon had a lifting power of 5 cwt and contained 37,000 cubic feet of gas

5 A balloon in the grounds of Brooker Hall, New Church Road, Brighton, *c.*1905

6 The Rev John Bacon and his daughter aloft over London in their balloon 'Shrewsbury', *c.*1900

"SHREWSBURY"

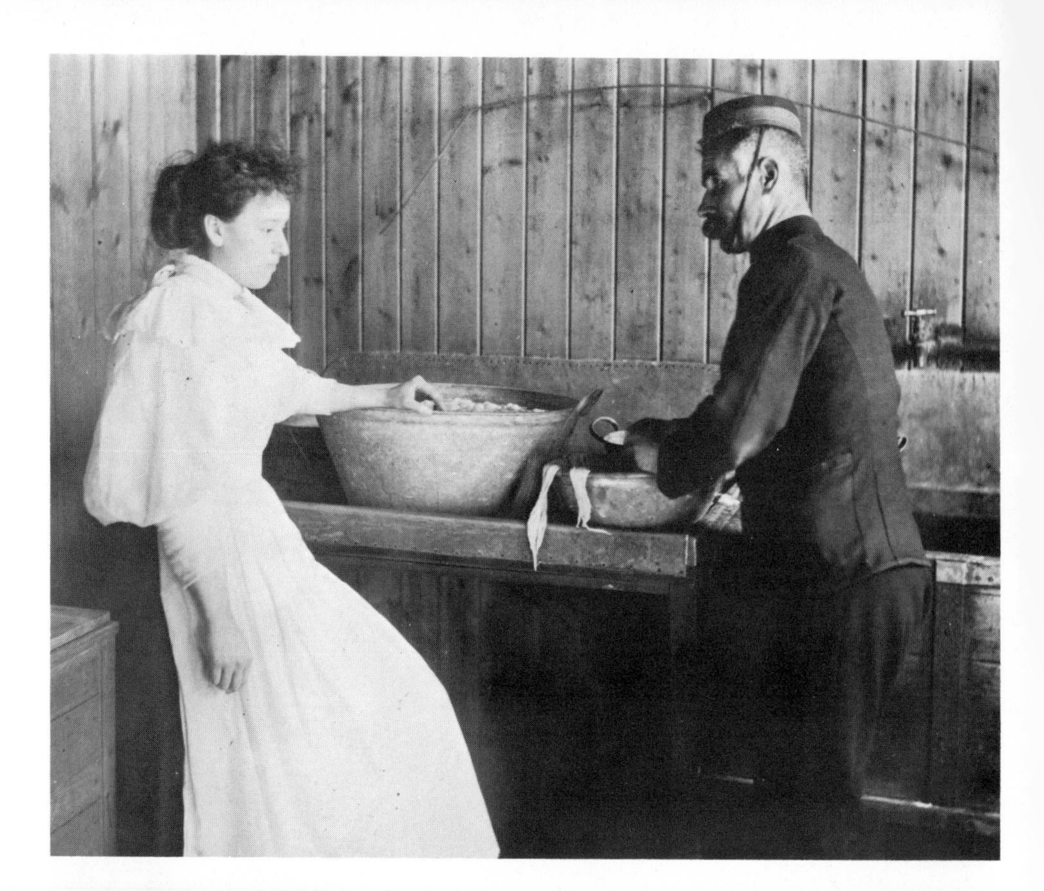

7 Preparing gold-beaters' skin in glycerine and water for balloon fabric, 1894

8 An early method of making hydrogen gas for balloons by the Royal Engineers, 1896

9 The Army Balloon Factory at Aldershot run by the Royal Engineers, 1898

10 *Left* A balloon ready to ascend, its retaining ropes held by Royal Engineers, 1896

11 *Above* Some 93 balloonists ascended from Hurlingham in May 1908. The winning post was Burchetts Green – west of Maidenhead – 30 miles distant

12 The Wellman balloon on display at the Aero-Exhibition, 1909. It was proposed to reach the North Pole. The envelope is being inflated

13 The fashionable being photographed at Hurlingham, 1910

14 From left to right: Rev. J.M. Bacon, Admiral Fremantle, Mr Fred Bacon and Mr Percival Spencer before their ascent in a balloon from Newbury Gas Works, July 1900. Their object was to further the use of balloons in war time

15 *Left* The start of the race for the Harbord Cup in May 1907 from Ranelagh. The winning post was Goring Railway Station

16 Emile Markeberg falling to his death from a balloon in July 1900

17 A balloon above Salisbury Plain, *c.*1890

18 The point-to-point balloon race at Hurlingham, June 1911, organised by the Royal Aero Club. The Hon. Mrs Assheton-Harbord in her balloon, North Star, piloted by Mr C.F. Pollock, ascending

19 Ballooning at Ranelagh, 1907. The destination of the race (communicated 'just before the ascent') was Goring-on-Thames. The winner 'descended within a hundred yards of the stake'

20 The Hedges-Butler cup at Hurlingham, July 1912. The North Star about to ascend with the Hon. Mrs Assheton-Harbord and her friends

21 A balloon ascent from Norwich Market Place, 22 June 1897, to celebrate Queen Victoria's Jubilee

22 An early air photograph of London, showing Whitehall, the Houses of Parliament and the Thames. The picture was taken *c.*1900 from the balloon of the Rev. John M. Bacon, whose daughter was the photographer (see **6**)

23 Balloon Club meeting at Ranelagh, 30 May 1908

24 Private balloon rising above the trees, *c.*1895

Airships

25 The airship 'Delta', July 1913. She was a Royal Aircraft Factory machine

26 The 'Nulli Secundus' flying at Farnborough Common, 1908. The balloon rose to 500 feet and flew for 25 miles

27 Army trials with an airship at Farnborough, 1908

28 The airship 'Beta', 1910, crewed by the Royal Navy. It ran into its shed at 65/70 feet in 1911

29 The first British airship 'Nulli Secundus', starting on its three-mile maiden flight from Aldershot, September 1907

30 The airship 'Parseval No. 4' being manoeuvred into its shed at Farnborough in February 1914

31 The airship 'Astra Torres'. She was Royal Navy Airship No. 3 and was purchased by R.N.A.S. in May 1913

32 The new Army airship 'Dirigible' No. 1, 1910

33 The first British aircraft to fly under power. It was 120 feet long and had a 50-hp Antoinette engine. The flight took place on 5 October 1907 and was from Farnborough to London. The machine was scrapped in September 1908

34 The airship 'Gamma' emerging from her shed at Aldershot, 1910

Lady Aeronauts

35 *Left* Armed with a megaphone and leaflets two suffragettes ascended in a balloon for the opening of Parliament, 1909

36 Wilbur Wright and his daughter about to ascend, March 1909

37 *Left* Claude Graham White and his fiancée, Miss Dorothy Taylor, 1912

38 The lady aviator's costume of 1911 modelled by Mrs Henlett at Brooklands

39 An American flying machine designed by Charles G. King. Here it is in England with Albert C. Grant and two ladies who were to make a flight with him, May 1911

Fatalities

40 The crashed wreck of the monoplane 'B258', lost in the Army manoeuvres of September 1912. Captain Hamilton and Lieutenant Wyness-Stuart were killed

42 The wrecked army airship 'Lebaudy' at Woodlands Cottage, Farnborough, the residence of Captain and Lady Follett, where it crashed in May 1911

41 An early crash. This one occurred in June 1910 and resulted in a broken neck for the pilot

43 The wreck of the military monoplane '263', which crashed near Oxford causing the death of Lieutenants Bettington and E.H. Hotchkiss, 1908

Navy and Army Flying

44 A balloon at the Royal Military Academy, Sandhurst. Cadets in their summer blazers and hats are on the left, *c.*1890

45 The No. 1 Balloon Section on military manoeuvres on Salisbury Plain, 1893. The white cover on the soldiers' helmets indicates their status as Friend or Foe

46 The traction engine and trailer belonging to the Royal Engineers Balloon division. Aldershot, 1908

47 *Above* Adjusting the valve of an Army balloon prior to filling, 1908

48 Filling a balloon from gas cylinders, 1908

49 Spreading a balloon prior to filling, 1908

50 The balloon being raised up. The gas apparatus can be seen in the cart, 1908

51 Tying the tail of an Army balloon, 1908

52 The Balloon Section of the Royal Artillery returning after 'free trailing' with a balloon, 1893. The balloon's basket can be seen

53 A free start from the garden of Colonel J. Cappers, Superintendent of the Army Balloon Factory, 1909

54 Men of the Royal Engineers starting off on a flight, 1909

55 The car and 70-hp engine of an Army airship, 1908

56 The car of the airship 'Astra Torres' with Royal Navy personnel, 1913

57 A Royal Engineers balloon taking off, 1909

58 A balloon being packed by Royal Engineers, 1896, on Laffans Plain

59 The swivelled propellers are in position for elevating the airship 'Delta' during Army manoeuvres in September 1912

60 Men of the Army Flying Corps repairing a damaged flying machine, August 1912

61 Members of the Army Flying Corps on Salisbury Plain during manoeuvres, August 1912. It is recorded that there were 'no fewer than 10 flyers in the air at one time soaring and swooping'. This monoplane had a broken propeller

62 The general staff watching the first fly past by the Royal Flying Corps, 1912

63 A lecture on aeroplanes given by Lieutenant Fox to the men of the 8th Battalion the Worcestershire Regiment (Territorials), August 1912

64 Army Flying Corps personnel during manoeuvres, *c.*1911, trying to repair a 'Henry Farman'

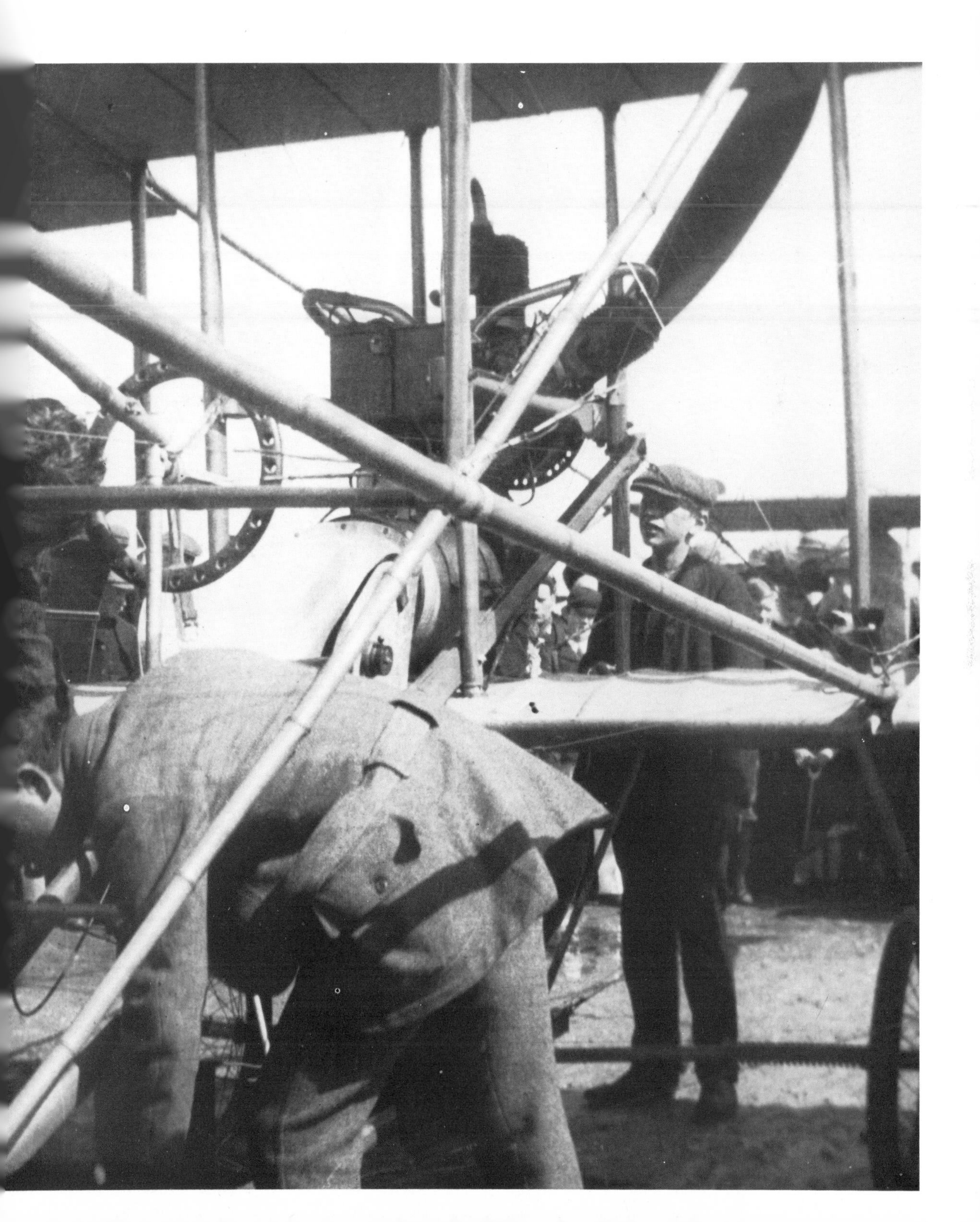

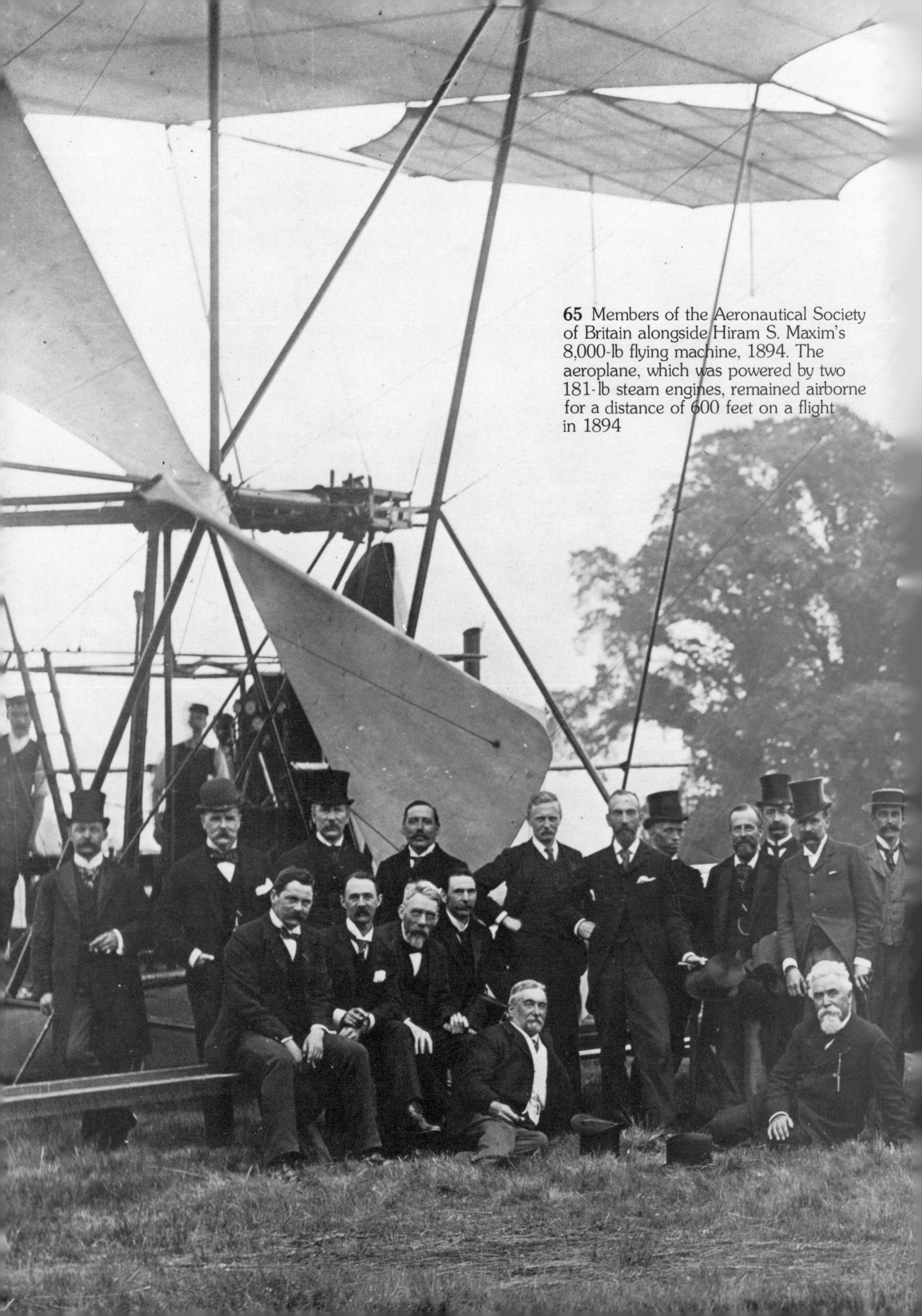

65 Members of the Aeronautical Society of Britain alongside Hiram S. Maxim's 8,000-lb flying machine, 1894. The aeroplane, which was powered by two 181-lb steam engines, remained airborne for a distance of 600 feet on a flight in 1894

Personalities

66 Colonel Templer of the Royal Engineers in a balloon car, 1894

67 Paul Cornu's experimental helicopter was the first in its field. This photograph of it was taken on 13 November 1909

68 The postman handing a letter bag to Gustave Hamel for the first air mail carried. The route was from Hendon to Windsor, a distance of 20 miles, and the year 1911

69 Geoffrey de Havilland in his second aircraft, FE1, at Farnborough. De Havilland tested aircraft for the Army at this time, 1910

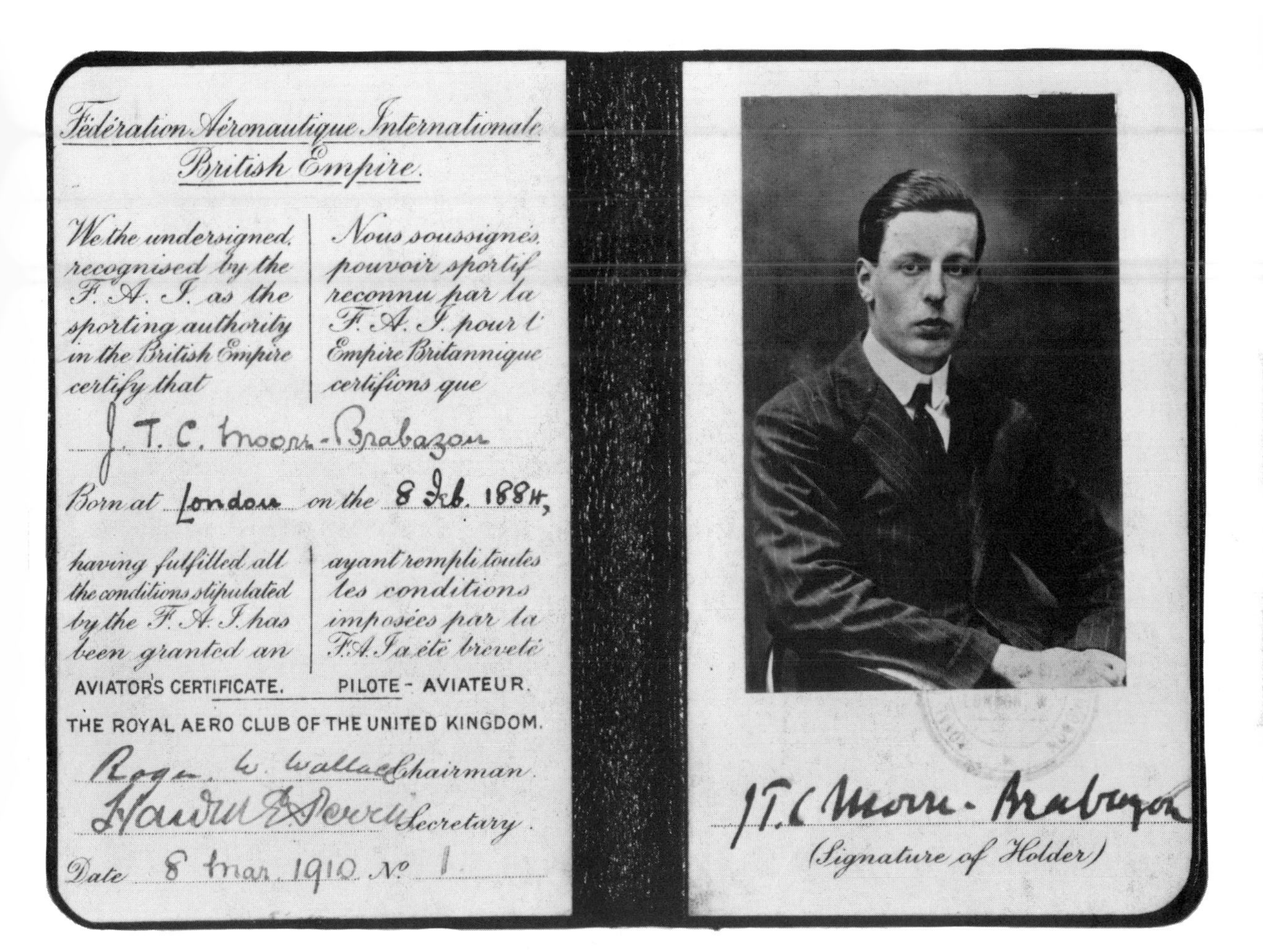
Fédération Aéronautique Internationale
British Empire.

We the undersigned, recognised by the F.A.I. as the sporting authority in the British Empire certify that	Nous soussignés, pouvoir sportif reconnu par la F.A.I. pour l'Empire Britannique certifions que

J.T.C. Moore-Brabazon

Born at London on the 8 Feb. 1884,

having fulfilled all the conditions stipulated by the F.A.I. has been granted an	ayant rempli toutes les conditions imposées par la F.A.I. a été breveté
AVIATOR'S CERTIFICATE.	PILOTE - AVIATEUR.

THE ROYAL AERO CLUB OF THE UNITED KINGDOM.

Roger W. Wallace Chairman

Harold E. Perrin Secretary

Date 8 Mar. 1910 No 1

J.T.C. Moore-Brabazon
(Signature of Holder)

70 The first pilot's licence, issued to J.T.C. Brabazon later Lord Brabazon of Tara, 8 March 1910

71 R. Sommer with the seven passengers who made a one-hour flight with him in April 1911

72 Gustave Hamel, who flew from Hendon to Hove at an altitude of 3,000 feet in April 1911. His machine was a 50-hp Blériot

73 Pierre Prier, who flew from London to Paris in under four hours without a stop. He is here photographed with a friend at Hendon, in his Blériot monoplane, April 1911

74 The Hon. C.S. Rolls with his balloon 'Britannia' and a group of friends from White's Club, London, after a three-hour trip, May 1907

75 The Hon. C.S. Rolls has his lifebelt adjusted before flying from Dover to Calais and back, June 1910

76 Colonel Cody at the controls of his biplane

77 King Alphonso XIII of Spain with Wilbur Wright on the Wright biplane, February 1909

78 King Edward VII inspecting the Wright biplane with Wilbur Wright, 1909

79 Winston Churchill in a Short No. 2 'School Machine', 1912. The Short Brothers originally manufactured balloons

Kites and Gliders

80 An Army 'D' pattern box-kite, 1909

81 Lawrence Hargrave's box kite, 1898. Invented in Australia in 1893, aeroplanes adopted its cellular principle

82 The Cody man-lifting kite with its telephone connection, aloft in Hampshire, 1904

83 An abortive attempt to get off the ground in the Fitzgerald flying machine at Trinity College Dublin, 1895

84 José Weiss, an Alsatian working and living in England with his flapping-wing glider, 1905. He later worked for Sir Frederick Handley-Page

85 Percy Pilcher's 'Bat' glider, 1895. He was killed flying 'The Hawk' glider in 1899

86 The 'D' pattern Army pilot kite, 1909

87 An Army kite smashed during a practice flight, 1905

88 A model of John Stringfellow's 'Ariel', which had a 20-foot wingspan and was powered by steam. It made one of the very first mechanical flights, 1848

89 The Short Brothers' S.3.9 'Triple Twin' 1911

Heavier than Air Power Machines

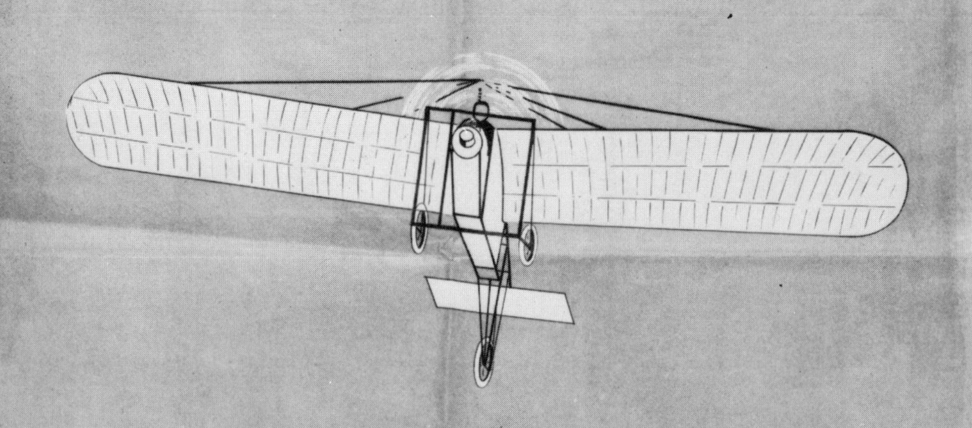

G. N. R.
ENGLAND'S FIRST AVIATION RACES
AT
DONCASTER
OCTOBER 15TH TO 23RD
SEE SPECIAL PROGRAMMES FOR TRAIN SERVICE & EXCURSION
ARRANGEMENTS GRATIS AT ANY GREAT NORTHERN OFFICE

90 The Great Northern Railway Company's poster advertising England's first aviation races, at Doncaster, 15-23 October 1909

91 The 30-hp engine of a Humber aeroplane at the Coventry Factory, 1910. The price was £450

92 S.F. Cody's biplane with its 120-hp Austro-Daimler engine. The machine wor £5,000 in military trials on Salisbury Plair 1912

93 *Right* A view of the Humber aeroplan factory in March 1910. Wings are being manufactured on the right, with carpenter at work in the background

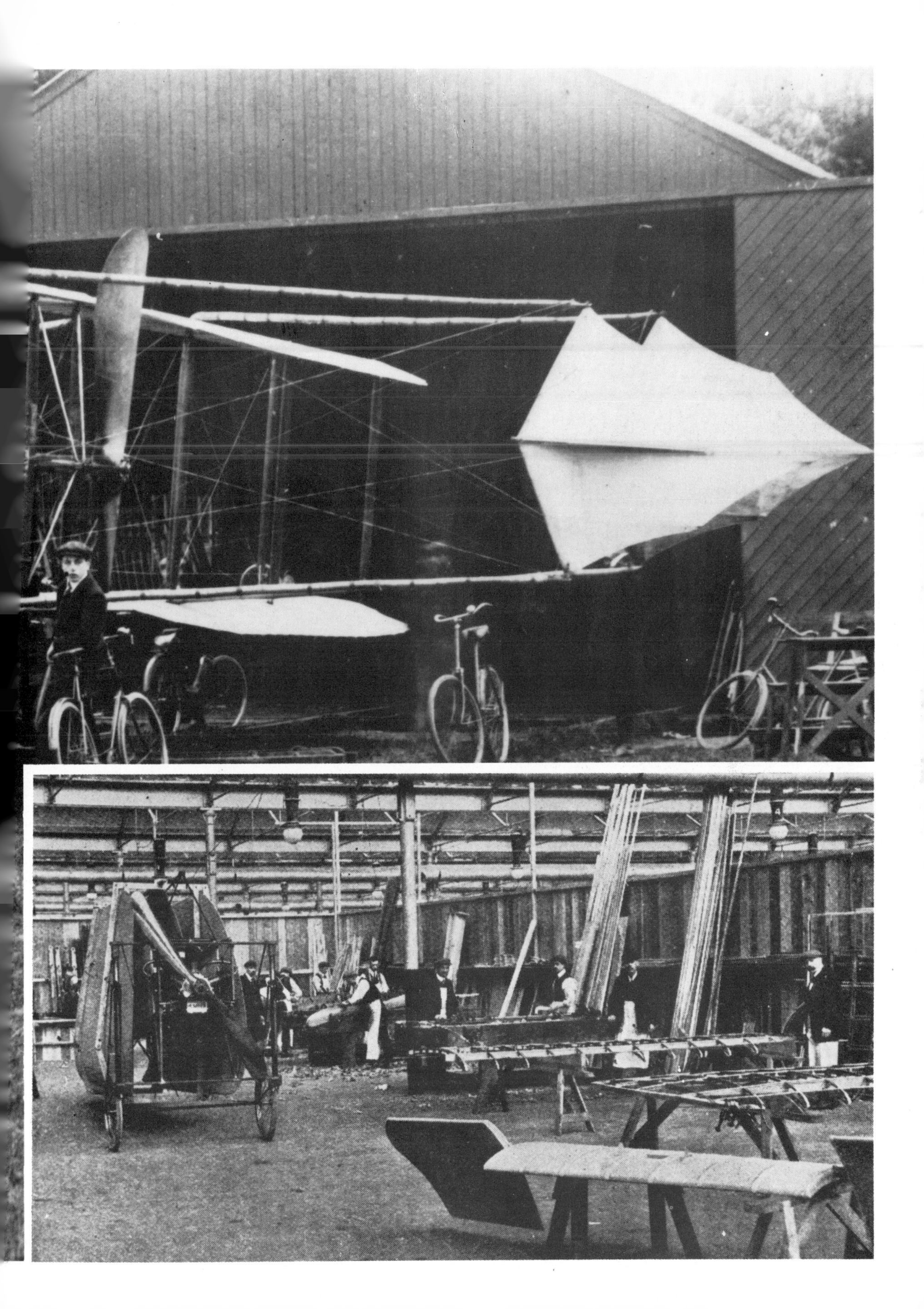

205

4 A B.E.2 tractor biplane of No. 2
quadron, Royal Flying Corps, at
ontrose, Scotland, 1913

95 The aviation workshop of Patrick Alexander, 1902. Alexander had been a recognised authority on the practical and theoretical aspects of flight since the 1880s

96 A Bristol 'box kite' at Five Oak Green, Tonbridge, Kent. It was built by Sir George White and the British and Colonial Aeroplane Company

97 The Etrich monoplane at Eastchurch, the naval aviation ground on the Isle of Sheppey, December 1912. The pilot was Lieutenant Reginald Gregory, R.N.

98 The race from Paris to London, July 1911. A prize of £2,500 was offered by *The Standard* to the winner. The picture shows M. Védrines, the first aviator to reach Hendon

99 B.C. Hucks in his Blériot monoplane 'Firefly', above Crowhurst Farm, Gorleston, Norfolk, on 3 August 1912

100 The folding-wing monoplane 'Marcey', December 1911. It was described as a 'flying beetle'

101 The Voisin hydro-aeroplane, 1912. It could carry seven passengers. The engine was in the boat and the power was conveyed by a chain

102 A monoplane crossing the channel in 1911 from Calais to Dover for a prize of 100 guineas offered by the 'Dover Committee'

140

103 Refreshment for the police at Hendon Aerodrome's inaugural meeting, July 1911

CROSSMAN & PAULIN
LIMITED
BREWERS.
LONDON.

104 The Short No. 1 aircraft, 1908. It had a Voisin motor car engine, but never flew

105 Blériot's monoplane, July 1911. It was a popular training aircraft with the Royal Flying Corps

106 *Right* The Sopwith dual control machine, 1914, in which Winston Churchill was taught to fly

107 A Blériot monoplane minus its wings at the inaugural meeting at Hendon Aerodrome, 1911

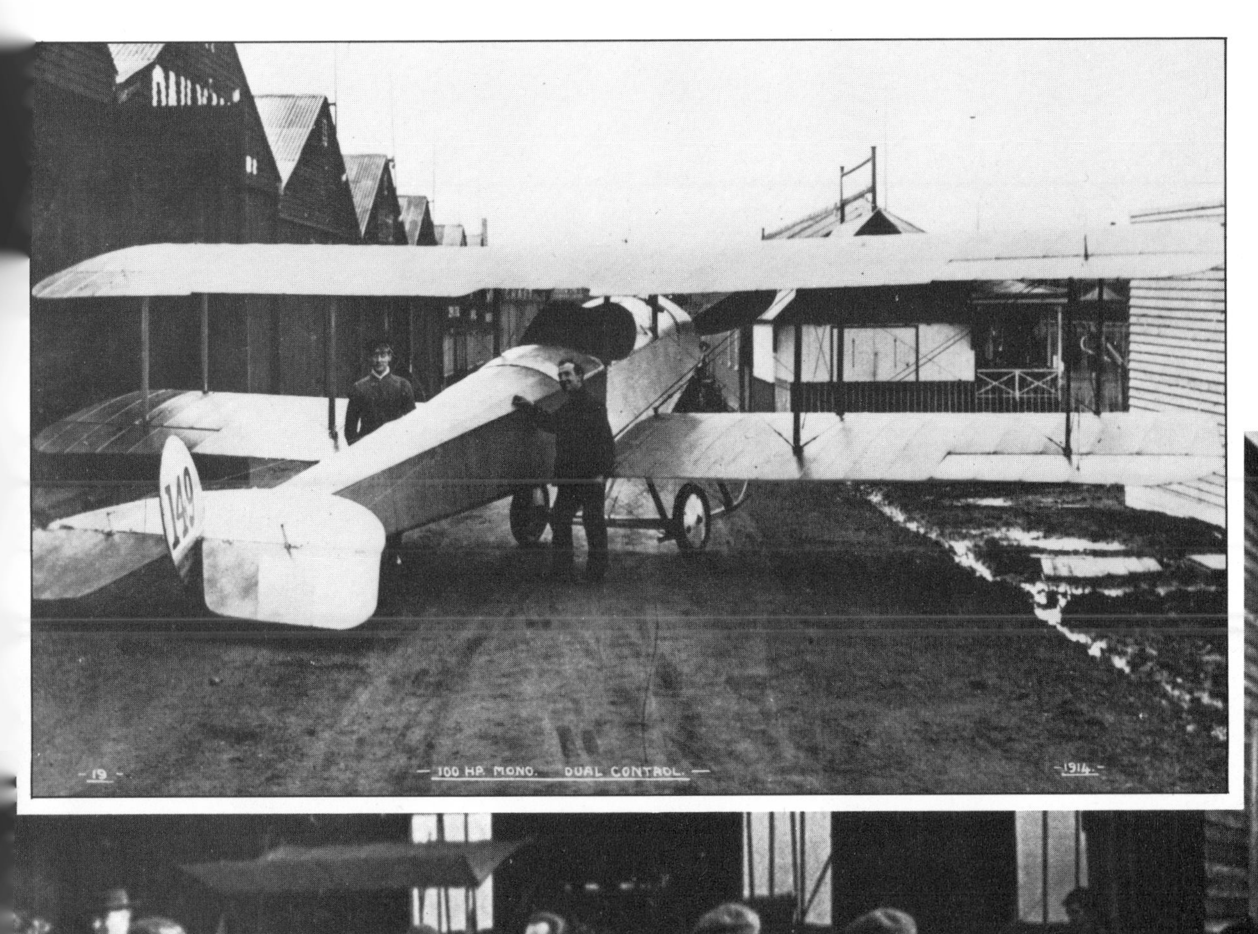
149
-19-
-100 HP. MONO. DUAL CONTROL.-
-1914.-

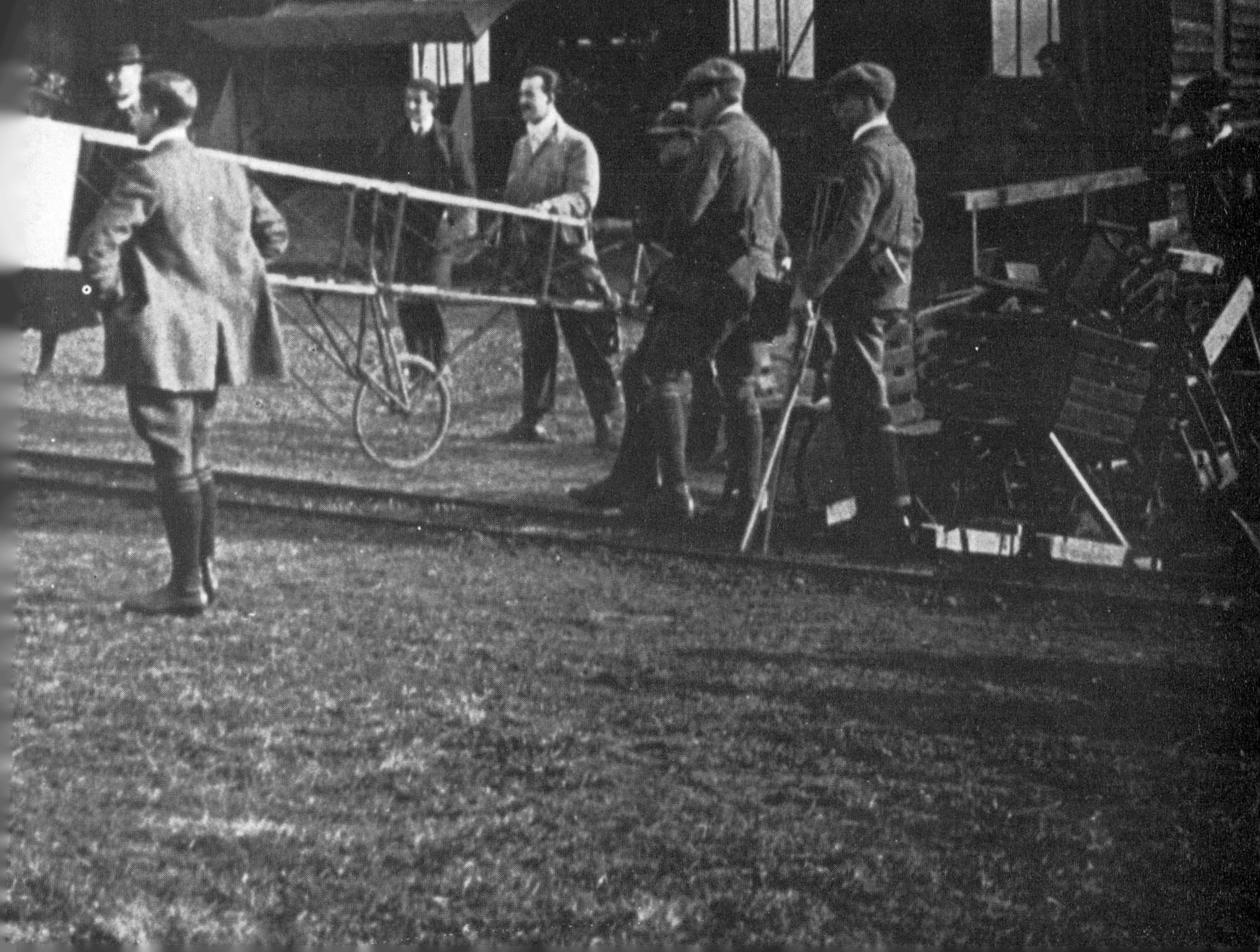

108 The Avro 500, a 2-seater biplane with a 50-hp Gnome engine, 1913

109 Commander Schwann R.N. with the experimental hydroplane built for the Royal Navy, 1911. It is here seen at Cavendish Dock, Barrow-in-Furness

110 F.K. McLean flying his Short tractor biplane through Tower Bridge, August 1912

111 The Short tractor hydro-biplane on the Thames, August 1912. It had just flown up the river from the Isle of Sheppey to Westminster Bridge

112 Cody's British Army aeroplane No. 1, 1908. It was powered by an engine borrowed from the airship 'Nulli Secundus'

113 The Valkyrie monoplane, July 1911, which carried for the British General Electrical Company a consignment of light bulbs from Shoreham to Hove. One of the first air cargo flights

114 A Prier-Dickson biplane No. 75(256) at Farnborough, 1913

115 A Henry Farman seaplane, 1912

116 The S.E.1 biplane at Aldershot